Essays

by the

Invisibles

Angelyn Ray

Essays by the Invisibles

ISBN: 9798606450343

Special Credit:

Adelaide Anne Procter
  for her poem, "The Lost Chord"

Contents

To the

Encompassing

Cloud of Witnesses

The I is the worm;
        the I Am is the moth.

The I is the caterpillar;
        the I Am is the butterfly.

The I is the hungry baby;
        the I Am is the happy baby.

The I is the missing;
        the I Am is the meeting.

NIKOLA TESLA

Were I to write an essay today, I would write of stars and galaxies, and I would write of blood flowing through your veins, enlivening your organs, and there would be no difference. For it is only in the vernacular of your day that there seems to be a difference between the flow of the universe and the flow of your wondrous bodies.

Do you have any idea what I am talking about? Emanuel Swedenborg said, "…the whole heaven resembles one man, which is therefore called the Greatest Man." Perhaps he will want his own essay, but for now, let me say that is what I am referencing: YOU are the micro, to the macro of the universe. No difference at all. Therefore, as you advance, so does the universe. There is no difference.

When you see death and destruction, and dismay and dis-gruntlement all about you, does that mean that you are dismayed and dis-gruntled, and deadly and destructive? No. Ordinarily, it does not mean that.

What it means is that the decayed and dying parts of you are sloughing away, scraping off of the livening parts of you that are burgeoning from within. When the rotted skins separate from the newly developing life within you, that new life needs exposure to the new atmosphere, the newly developing environment, so that it can withstand those rarefied rays and radiances. So the old must be scraped away or the exposure of the new cannot occur, and it will soon be infected by the old.

So know that, when you see the death and destruction in the macro, and the rot and decay all around you, around this dear Earth, among the peoples hereof, what is happening in the micro, in you, is exactly the same – not that you are decaying, but the death of the old you – the old and obsolete parts of you – are slipping off, falling away. There is soreness, tenderness, as the new is exposed for the first time. That is what you are feeling, and it is for a good cause, a very, very good cause.

When all the old sloughs off, and all the new is all there is of you, you will not see the decay and rot in the universe around you. For the macro faithfully

13

mirrors the micro, just as the micro faithfully mirrors the macro.

Only the manifestation differs somewhat for everyone, for while there is a uniformity among all, there is a uniqueness about each. Each one of you reflects the whole in a slightly different manner, and the whole reflects back to you in that unique manner, unique in all.

And in that is delight, never a dull moment, as "they say," for, as at a costume party, there is a steady parade of custom-made manifestations of that "Greatest Man," or we should say that "Greatest Human," never two the same, and even in that, one is never quite the same from day to day. Constant creativity; constant creation.

These are the thoughts I bring to this essay. There is more!

There is an emptiness when the old sloughs away, for one is accustomed to it. Just as when one puts away the winter wardrobe as Spring takes hold and the days begin to warm and widen, one may fondly clean and fold the sweaters and lay them carefully in the cedar chest – one may have fond memories of the olden times.

But the cedar chest is closed. And what if the next wintertime doesn't arrive? Does one mourn if the summertime leads on to a yet brighter time, unanticipated, unexpected? Does one cry over the unused, unneeded sweaters? Perhaps, and if so, one can always go back into another winter.

In other words, can you adapt to a brighter, lighter time than you are accustomed to? than you have ever known? Can you embrace it as you might embrace a new baby, or perhaps an angel, who suddenly arrives at your doorstep and rings your bell?

This is less an essay and more a challenge, do you say? Is it a welcome challenge? That is the question. Your answer depends upon your readiness to put down your old customs and ways and enter into new and creative ways and joys.

The weather, too, answers to the changes and the challenges taking place, within both the micro and the macro. And still it does conform somewhat to the seasonal changes which you are accustomed to. Yet there are upheavals, and unseasonal blasts, storms and lulls, events that surprise and change one's outlook and routines. These are signs that one is entering unaccustomed and unfamiliar areas of being, in the micro sense.

Take them as such – take the whims and changes and challenges on the weather fronts as signs that YOU are changing on the inner front – that the vanguard within you is advancing. Know that it is a good thing if you can see it and receive it as such.

In other words, can you find joy within yourself in spite of what you find outside yourself? Can you find peace within? Can you feel love? If you find these blessed qualities in the midst of unfamiliar circumstances and an environment that you are not accustomed to, it means that you have already created them within – or rather retrieved them from the eternal well of goodness that is always at your fingertips.

Or – if you do not find them within, it is time for you to create them within – or rather retrieve them from the eternal well of goodness that is still at your fingertips. Or, if not at your literal fingertips, at the tip of your mind, at the top of your awareness.

The well of wellness and well-being is always available, only sometimes you see it and sometimes you don't. It is the epitome of creativity to find it when you do not feel it – or to feel it when you do not find it.

Either way, finding it or feeling it, which is one and the same, self-determines the way ahead, determines the environment into which you are advancing, the being into which you are growing, as you let the new emerge from within while the old falls away.

The I is the ring;
the I Am is the sphere.

The I is the ground;
the I Am is the world.

The I is the seagull;
the I Am is the sea.

The I is the bracelet;
the I Am is the arm.

H YPATIA

I frequent the depths when I want to go deep.

When I want to be lit, I go to the sun.

Or I sit quietly and let the sun come to me. And it always does!

Why shouldn't it?

"Why should it?" you say. "The sun never comes to anyone."

Ah, but surely you have felt the sun resting on your shoulders, and the sun-infused sands beneath your feet. How could the sands burn if the sun had not come to them, lighted on them, lighted them?

So the sun comes to one who calls upon it to come to them.

Will it burn? Only if the call is insincere, or if it is an attempt to test the sun.

I frequent the treetops. I travel on the invisible webs spun there by the levitating arachnids, who go from treetop to treetop, weaving together all the trees in the forest, and as surely, even from forest to forest.

For it is not enough that the trees are all joined invisibly under the ground, their roots reaching and coaxing and cajoling the company of one another until they are all intertwined in a slow subterranean dance of recognition. It is no surprise to them – it is their secret. It only surprises us when we learn of it.

We think of the underground cities as though they are made up of creatures recognizable to us – as if they bear some sort of likeness to us. What if it is the interweaving and the intertwining of all the tree roots that comprise those underground bustling *metropoleis*? And why couldn't it be?

Because you think the denizens of those sub-earthly realms ought to be related to us? But they are, for the trees are our symbiotic counterparts. Have you not heard that our breathing depends upon their output? And their breathing depends upon our output?

Now if we are to descend further into the bowels of the earth, we would find creatures of a design not so inter-dependent with ours. That is, no symbiosis. That is, further, no symbiosis that is recognizable to us – to them perhaps, or perhaps not. Recognizable to some among them, to others, not.

So, do you think that I only frequent the heights? And the depths? Then you are mistaken! For I never frequent the heights, or the depths! I only use those terms so that you can relate to me, so that you can perceive a modicum of what I assay to say.

When I am at the heights, such as in the sun, or lingering about the treetops, and when I am in the depths, as under the sea or in the bowels of the earth, the truth is that I am in the midst. Just as you stand in the midst of your horizon, never at the edge, so, wherever I may lodge my awareness, I am in the midst.

For wherever there is a height, there is always a higher height, and wherever there is a depth, there is always a deeper deep, a depth that goes yet deeper than the one I am frequenting.

So, when I speak in terms of heights, or of depths, I am luring and cajoling my readers to explore their own. For when they reach the height to which they aspire, or the depth they wish to explore, they will find that there is more to be found above the height, and more to be plumbed, beneath the deep.

Deeper and higher, and eventually all will be known, all will be perceived. And that is when the adventure begins. I am tasting it; I am venturing there. When I have truly entered it you will not hear from me, until you have ventured there too.

It is only while I still have heights to explore, and depths to investigate, that I can come into your worlds and commune with you.

So you can see by this that there are many who do not commune with you, though your ways and means are open books to them. Yet their ways and means are not open to you, until you have searched out your own heights and depths.

And you must understand that the depths I frequent, and the sun, and the treetops of which I have spoken, while real and substantial, are metaphors for the depths and the heights, and the wide spaces within yourself – within yourselves. It is these that you must enter and explore, turning over every leaf, every iota, getting to know every breath and every breeze. That is the work you are undertaking – if it is your pleasure to do so – and that is how you will arrive at the beginning of the true adventure. For now you are gathering the gear, equipping yourself, yourselves, for that eventuality.

It is a bustling work, an exciting world, that you occupy, and the more you see it so, the more you can enthuse as you traverse the byways and absorb all the surprises along the way, without fear, with anticipation and expectation of an accelerating joy and enthusiasm, for the unfolding wonders that lie yet before you, directly in your path, and directly within you.

Will I miss the camaraderie we have shared here, when I enter my own adventure, having completed my foray into the heights and the depths to which

I have merely alluded here? Will I miss you?

No. Not at all! Because I will still be able to look in and see, see how you are coming along, for your ways and means will be open books to me then, more completely than now, far more so.

Furthermore, I will see the end of your coming into your own adventures, the assurance of it, of all of it, for I will not see you sitting by the side of the road waiting for a ride, or even speeding along on your way. I will be seeing the entire road you travel, and have traveled, and yet will travel, and it will be as if you are already there, already having joined me there in the eternity of the great adventures.

The I is the dream;
            the I Am is awakening.

The I is the word;
            the I Am is creation.

The I is the leaving;
            the I Am is the arriving.

The I is the eye;
            the I Am is the seeing.

EMANUEL SWEDENBORG

Do not find it intimidating, the fact that there are societies who call themselves by my name, and that you are not too familiar with them. Or yet, that the "voice" with which you speak may seem to be the same among the essayists here – a natural thing. For the themes are different, and bespeak an individuality within the unity.

For I daresay that when it is done, there will be a unity among all our themes, like areas in a jigsaw puzzle which, without the picture of the finished puzzle as a pattern to go by, will seem to contain unrelated areas. So we each have our area and when put together, will comprise a whole.

What, then, is my theme?

We could say that Nikola Tesla's is the micro and the macro, and Hypatia's is the heights and the depths, could we not?

Let us then label my theme as the spirit and the matter. A play on words, perhaps, with spirit being a liveliness and matter a heaviness. Or with spirit being an elusive invisibility, and matter an evident tangibility. What shall I say, then, on the "matter"?

I was known in my span of human life with the label you know me by – Emanuel Swedenborg – as communing with spirits as though it were a natural occurrence, and with bringing wisdom from that realm of reality. For the world of spirit is a realm, and it is real. In fact, it is composed of many realms, each real in its own manner of manifestation.

It is like a galaxy, which is named as a singularity, an object, while a galaxy is actually a plurality composed of numberless components. So the realm of spirit comprises numberless areas for exploration by that intrepid pioneer, the very one who ventures into the unseen unknown, with courage befitting the hardiest voyager.

If you think the Earth houses a great variety of species, some undiscovered as yet, and all collected under the label of the materially tangible, think of the truly unimaginable scope of possibilities strewn, not across the universe, but among all the intangible universes!

No wonder the Father has many mansions!

No wonder the Mother has many children! Children to inhabit the many mansions!

But when I see "mansions" in my mind, and "children," I do not see only earthly abodes and human beings. I see the variety that stretches beyond all earthly imaginings in infinite directions. Not only an infinite variety, but also the directions where they are to be found are of an infinitude.

We said my theme would be the spirit and the matter, but now I wish to segue into a different path of pursuit. It is as familiar as your own heart, or perhaps more familiar (many not knowing their own hearts, or else explored only in fits and starts). What is that path of pursuit?

It is the free will. For to venture into the "galaxies" of spirit exploration would overwhelm and inundate one, or catch one in an endless series of eddies, each eddy harder to leave than the last, if one is not free to will, free to determine one's own steps and movements – when and how to enter – how to remain – and when and how to exit each and every "room" one enters.

This is prerequisite to one's explorations and forays into that infinitude of spirit and the universes – the uni-verses – the single songs – of each. The choices and the options are endless – endless. Truly without end.

Mainly, in regard to the free will of each individual, without its fullest development, there is no freedom at all. So the theme of "free will" segues quickly into that of freedom. One should define it.

Freedom, developed from "free will," is a clear path, without obstructions, without unwanted detours, and without dead ends. It is a clear path WITH tributaries, forks, intersections, and byways that allow for the fullest and most fulfilling excursions "to one's heart's content."

Do you see why I bring up the subject of the free will of the human being? The fully developed free will, knowing all the choices, how to choose, how not to choose (choosing against a certain course of action), sets the gears for how one will navigate in the endless worlds of spirit.

The free will is tested and tried. Decisions are forced upon one so that every person has to choose, and even if not choosing, a course of action, or inaction, is undertaken. It is upon these choices, or lack of choices, that one's eternal heritage hinges.

I am not here at this time, and on this page, to tell of my own forays into the worlds of spirit. Rather, I am here to assure you that every test you receive, every forced and unforced choice you make, directly sets your course for your forays – their quality, nature, and extent – into realms beyond this life.

Is the Earth under a quarantine, as some have said? Perhaps. If it is a negatively derived imprisonment, there is all the more reason to develop one's free will to its finest capacity, to hone it to its sharpest incisiveness.

And, again, if it is a negatively derived imprisonment, one's free will – if tuned to the finer overseeing spirits who allow, thus oversee, the negatively derived prison – will bring one to that realm of oversight, to the learning beyond the quarantine.

For that is an essential characteristic of "free will" – it can reach beyond any constraint put on it – as long as it reaches into the realm of spirit, over-coming the gravity that binds one to matter, to tangible materiality.

Many of my followers have searched for the quality in me that opened and allowed my extraordinary ventures and adventures into the realms of the spirit, and it is – or was – just that. It was a highly developed "free will," so that I could come and go from and to those realms and not lose myself somewhere along the way.

Rather, I was able coherently and cogently to order my path among the byways of the spiritual worlds, and to return to this tangible human realm and relate my findings.

A mundane message I have brought, but there is nothing mundane about the implications and the hidden meanings abundantly provided "between the lines" for the intrepid, diligent pioneer and voyager.

Trevlig resa! (Bon voyage!)

The I is the egg;
          the I Am is the peacock.

The I is the epitaph;
          the I Am is the essence.

The I is the note;
          the I Am is the symphony.

The I is the pan;
          the I Am is the bread.

MIRRA ALFASSA

I am known in Wikipedia as "a spiritual guru, an occultist and a collaborator of Sri Aurobindo, who considered her to be of equal yogic stature to him and called her by the name 'The Mother.'"

Well, that is what they say, and I suppose there is some truth in it.

My own most meaningful role during those times, when I was known by that name, was the invisible closeness which I held with many of the disciples of that day – disciples of Sri

Aurobindo. He could not be both father and mother to the followers, so he chose me to fulfill the mother role. And we both learned how hungry they all were for a mother!

Yet the mothering was not a physical nurturing – they were taught to do that for themselves – it was a nurturing of the soul, and the inner, invisible parts of them that were so often neglected, or completely ignored. Yet, like the pineal gland, though it may shrivel and suffer, it remains.

The shriveling and suffering parts of the human beings around me, which could not be fed with proverbial table scraps or even with sumptuous feasting, woke up and sought me out to feed those parts. And what was the result?

Since those parts – the inner, invisible, "soul" parts – are not born at the physical birth and do not die at the physical death, I became "mother" sometimes before a birth, and often after a death. I was able to escort and accompany, and comfort, those parts when they were separated from the body at death.

And those parts knew me and recognized me as one who knew them and comforted them while they were still encased in the body, and they willingly and gratefully counted on my support and succor after the encasement ended. They counted on me to help ease the transition, as one familiar both in the body and out of it, and to help point the way forward and onward when the transition time slipped into the time for progress.

I still fulfill that role for many, only now it is from my own "inner, invisible" resources, rather than from a place of my own physical encasement.

Now, for those who read these words, both in and out of their physical bodies, I will share some wisdom that I have gleaned during these works.

It is said, "Go to the light." And it is said, "Do not go to the light." Or to go to a certain light and not to another certain light.

Sometimes it is beneficial to go into a darkness – not an external darkness, but into the pregnant womb within one's own self (male or female, both have this womb). The womb is a dark place, and so is the earth when one is in a cave, or for the plants who dwell there and do not spring out until it is the season to do so.

Do not be afraid to go into a darkness when it is felt to be "safe."

How does one know if it is safe? The same way one knows if the light is safe or unsafe. It is nearly always learned while one is in the body, for then one is in a state of free will. And it can only be known by searching the inner, invisible spaces.

Do you know what I mean by "spaces"? Not "space" as in the physical universe, but "space" as in the realms within oneself. So safety, or the lack of safety, hence danger, can only be determined by going within, within the discerning depths of one's own being.

When one dies, one goes into a "cocoon." From the outside, a cocoon appears enclosed, but from the inside, many dreams happen, many worlds are spun, more than can be spun when one is outside and not within a cocoon.

When one can recognize one's own cocoon, spun about at the time of one's death, one will know whether or not there is a "light" to go to, and just which "light" is the most beneficial (for all hold benefit of some kind, for learning hard lessons if nothing else), or whether to rest in a dark womb or cave of some sort. Just as in the body one is accustomed to the gifts both of the daylight and of the nighttime, there are gifts to be taken both in the light and the dark when the body is shed.

Since every person's needs and situations differ from every other's, only general guidelines can be offered in a book for a general readership.

Therefore, it is especially imperative that each person knows what is within, what the needs are, what the propensities are and, chiefly, what is one's relationship with oneself. For only within can the next steps be determined.

There is another wisdom I have gleaned throughout the time of my absorbing work, which I will share with readers. This concerns one's relationships with others, and it may seem quite brazen at first glance.

Relationships with others – even the relationship many had with me as I helped them after their transitions out of the body were accomplished – can be considered mere measuring devices, measuring what is the true relationship with the self. It sounds eminently selfish, saying such a thing, and of course that is not the entire picture, only one tile in a great mosaic, yet a crucial piece.

Of a truth, one's relationships with others are measuring devices, measuring what is the true relationship with the self. Dwell on this, apply it to your own experience, and the meaning will grow on you.

Further, as you do this, you will find that your relationships with others are smoothing out and becoming more beneficial to them, and to yourself as well. And this is not to mention the healing of the relationship with the self that is at issue.

That is all I have to offer at this time, except to tie the pieces together thus: One's afterlife destiny is foreshadowed by the relationships one carries on during a human lifespan. Does it sound over-simple? Perhaps, because it is. The simplicity of a ruby, or of a rose, or a constellation.

The I is the coin;
              the I Am is the purchase.

The I is the spade;
              the I Am is the garden.

The I is the acorn;
              the I Am is the oak.

The I is the tunnel;
              the I Am is the open sky.

FARRAH FAWCETT

There comes a time when one wants to turn back to those one left, look in on them and share oneself, as one was able to do before the body was left behind.

It is not that the sharing and the looking in cannot be done at any time the departed soul is ready, a readiness that can occur immediately upon leaving the body behind, or some time afterward, or even, perhaps, never.

Now that I have spoken up and reserved a space for an "essay" in this book, I would like to pause for a bit and consider the most salient points I would like to record.

There! The pause that refreshes…

I would like to talk about beauty in its different forms, its effect in the various "worlds," and how better to utilize it, in any world.

A "world" as I speak of it is a given set of scenarios and factors that make up a complete environment within which a soul, embodied or not, finds its version of reality. For instance, one enters different "worlds" when one sleeps and dreams, while one is still in the same body. New environs are presented all the time in the dreaming state, hence, in the terms I am using, new worlds.

Now, beauty is to be found in any world, for "beauty is in the eye of the beholder." If one is capable of seeing beauty, one will find it. Some are incapable, and if that is the case, they see no beauty, no matter if they are surrounded by it.

Why is it important to learn to see it, if one finds oneself incapable, that is, if one does not or cannot perceive beauty in any form?

Take for instance a new baby. Some see only beauty in a newborn. Some see none. Most people recognize beauty in a rose; for those incapable of seeing beauty, they may objectify it, such as, "If I send her these roses she may look upon me favorably," or one may see only the potential of thorns that often accompany roses.

So then, why is it important to grow the ability to see beauty?

If one does not do this, one sets oneself up to inhabit only ugly worlds. For whatever we set up for ourselves is

what we will experience. Seeing
ugliness and ignoring beauty that is all
around us brings on more ugliness, and
more, in ever-varying forms. For all of
life is a set-up – what we set up for
ourselves.

We perceive set-ups that others
may create for us, not realizing that
their set-up is our opportunity to
recognize within it our own set-up for
ourselves.

If we perceive another's set-up –
whether it be from an individual such as
a spouse, teacher, parent, or another, or
whether it be from a political system or
set of laws, or the ubiquitous belief
systems found in other institutions – as
though we are a victim to that set-up,
we will never free ourselves from it.

That is why it is imperative that
when experiencing a set-up that was put

upon us by someone else, we recognize our own set-up within it. For only then do we retrieve the power that resides within us, to change the set-up to something else of our own choosing.

But let's back up for a minute. What about the person who cannot see beauty in any form, beauty for its own sake? Very likely that one learned to ignore, or even disdain beauty, for a good reason.

What if, as a child, there was a mother who was known as a great beauty, and who flaunted that beauty, convincing the child that s/he will never reach such a standard of beauty as the mother has already reached? What if that mother mistreated that child? The child learns that beauty harms and hurts, and sets up herself – or himself – to eschew beauty in any form. A beautiful rose reminds that growing person of the ugliness that overrode the visible beauty of the mother.

In that scenario, it is imperative that as the hurt child grows into an adult, and is able to assess his or her own set-ups, that set-up is recognized and replaced with one that allows beauty to penetrate and alter the person.

Altering the person presents a new question. How does beauty alter one? Simply by allowing one to see beauty in oneself. Seeing beauty in oneself, as opposed to seeing ugliness, or mere plainness, is necessary to finding beauty when one leaves one's body.

Does this mean that one must find physical, bodily beauty in oneself? It helps, but not necessarily. There is an old adage, "Beauty is only skin deep."

But I would say that beauty is beneath the skin and may radiate out through the skin, through the body from within, regardless of the body's current form. The body can be beautiful or ugly; still beauty can radiate out from within.

This radiation, or radiance, occurs when there is beauty to be found within. If the radiant one recognizes the beauty within, then so much the better, for that one will also recognize that it is not a matter of one creating one's own beauty, but rather a pre-existent beauty coming through one.

No rose would think itself the original and sole creator of its beauty, rather, it would know that it is the transmitter of a pre-existent beauty, though giving it a new form. So in this light, one may recognize the beauty that glows through oneself.

In that recognition lies one's ability to enter worlds that contain beauty, and eventually to enter worlds that contain only beauty. What better reason could there be than that, to enhance one's ability to ferret out beauty in any scenario while one is still in one's body?

So there is truth to the saying, "Beauty is in the eye of the beholder." One can train one's eye to behold beauty, and it will change not only one's present world, but all worlds to come for that one.

The I is the zygote;
        the I Am is the sage.

The I is the blade of grass;
        the I Am is the meadow.

The I is the snowflake;
        the I Am is the whited prairie.

The I is the tile;
        the I Am is the mural.

SACAJAWEA

I was raised in a culture where we were always at the center of the world. No matter where we found ourselves, that place was the center of the world, or you could say, the center of the universe.

This mindset conditioned us to be centered at all times, and to come from a place of centeredness, no matter what circumstances we were confronted with, and no matter what imbalance prevailed without.

And in my time, in my culture, there was plenty of imbalance around us, with which to contend. There were vicissitudes galore, coming from inclement weather, from scarcity of foodstuffs, though sometimes there was an overabundance, and we sought ways to preserve food at those times, and were often successful.

There was also imbalance in others, among the people in our tribe, who perceived the centeredness in which we dwelt to belong to themselves rather than to all. In other words, the imbalances and neuroses you find in your world today were not absent in ours.

Nevertheless, the standard held. Wherever we found ourselves, we were at the center of all things. If we held to the highest interpretation, we were centered; if we held to a lower interpretation, we were out of balance, and of course the degree of the imbalance corresponded to the degree of our misinterpretation of the meaning of being, always, at the center of the world.

May I tell you how I interpreted the standard of centering, and how my interpretation impacted both my own life, and the flow of history?

As to history, it would have played out regardless of my part, yet it is equally true that my own use of the philosophy of the centeredness of all things dovetailed with the flow that was occurring around me, and the larger dilemma that loomed for our peoples – that of the incursion of a body of people from another world – for so the coming of the European explorers was to us, an invasion that might as well have come from outer space.

I understood the meaning of being at the center of all things. I was also well aware of the failure of that philosophy, which, as most if not all philosophies, is only as true and useful as the one who adopts it.

In my own life I strove to utilize the philosophy in its highest manifestation, which was to view myself as sovereign, yet serving all about me. I saw that as the best use of the power that I inherently wielded, by virtue of my having a place in the human race, and in my specific tribe.

So when I was sold, to me the encircling horizon had closed in and my place at the center of the world had diminished as if in a moment. Still I was at the center.

Then when the opportunity arose for me to accompany the invaders to a distant land, and upon learning that I would be useful to them, the horizon opened up again, but onto a different world than I had known before. So once again I was at the center of my own world, and I claimed it as such, and tried to cherish it.

It is good to cherish one's world, the world within which one finds oneself, but it is not good to cherish it overmuch. A little cherishing helps to ease the trials, when the sovereignty clashes with the servitude – when the sense of one's sovereign self which is provided by being at the center, and one's sense of serving all that surrounds one because one is at the center – when those two senses, or roles, are at odds. Then a little cherishing of one's dual roles can ease the divide and help bring unity between the roles.

But overmuch cherishing, when the cherishing overcomes the realism of the central position and the tasks that result, binds one as if to a stake, and eventually there will be a burning. Such is the nature of overdone cherishing. Who will light the fire? The fire is already lit, by the overmuch cherishing. Thus, it behooves one to overcome the excessive cherishing before the flame begins to engulf one, even the hem of one's garment, or the toes of one's shoes.

So I advocate centering but not so much cherishing, which is like salt – a little goes a long way. Too much, and the whole meal is ruined.

It will help to order one's world if one does adopt the philosophy that one is always at the center of one's world, but only one's own. And from that central position one looks all around and sees how one can exercise her or his sovereignty in that world, to bring to bear the sovereign gifts, which one inherently holds, to improve that encircling environment, what is nearest one, and what is nearest the further reaches, out to the horizon.

Then a little cherishing. But first, the centering.

The I is the feather;
                    the I Am is the stork.

The I is the hair;
                    the I Am is the braid.

The I is the star;
                    the I Am is the Milky Way.

The I is the flame;
                    the I Am is the sun.

RUDOLF STEINER

Eurythmy. It was the greatest work that I accomplished. Yet many do not know of it, do not even know what it was, or what the word means. "The word *eurythmy* stems from Greek roots meaning beautiful or harmonious rhythm."

Today, eurythmyonline.com tells us: "Eurythmy was envisioned in the early 20th century by Dr. Rudolf Steiner, a visionary scientist of the spirit, whose mission it was to forge a fully conscious path of the spirit for the modern human being."

According to the Kamaroi Rudolf Steiner School: "Unique to Steiner schools, Eurythmy is a technique for integrating the arts and academic learning. Primarily an art of movement, Eurythmy encompasses elements of music, language arts and literature, speech and drama, geometry, and spatial and social awareness."

And to round out our definition of eurythmy, from Steiner.edu:

"Eurythmy is an art of human movement set to music, poetry, or speech. It is sometimes called 'speech made visible' and is intended to be a complement to intellectual learning. By studying eurythmy, students learn dexterity of movement, grace, poise, balance, and concentration."

Eurythmy has been considered a form of dance, and it is, but only insofar as eurythmy and modern dance, or shall we say ballroom dancing, engage the entire body in movement.

There are more differences than similarities between ballroom dancing and the movements utilized in the practice of eurythmy. We have just stated the similarity, that of the engagement of the entire body in movement.

The differences could be illustrated as follows:

Modern dance is the expression of the music which accompanies it. The music utilized in ballroom dancing plays a key role in the nature of the dance. The human dancer hears the music and sets the body to motion, led by the music.

In eurythmy, the impetus to movement comes not from an external source, from the orchestra, or the band, or the recording, or the singer, which are all tangible agents existing in the material world, the same world that is experienced by the dancer.

Rather, in eurythmy, the music is an accompaniment, a gentle escort, handing off the practicing eurythmist to the sacred communion that is occurring between the practitioner and the archetype, which is being awakened by the movements. The impetus to movement comes from intangible, archetypal sources, which are implanted in all but recognized by only the very few. The physical movements are expressive of deeply held roots in the cosmos, with correspondences to the most deeply held impulses within – the soul of the Cosmos communing with the soul of the individual being.

From the Great Oak School: "...the beautiful, spiritual and emotional art of eurythmy introduces students to the frameworks underlying speech and music through movement." And from Bestplacesofinterest.com/eurythmy:

"Eurythmy is speech and music made visible through conscious movements of the limbs. Eurythmy uses for its expression the most flexible of all instruments, the human body. Eurythmy knows no limitations in its possibility for the development of the body, mind and soul. Sounds contain wisdom, laws and mystery of the universe."

The best thing I can add to the descriptions that have been brought into this century is that the human body without the practice of eurythmy is like a fine violin that gets removed from its case now and then to be strummed a bit, maybe shown off, but not kept in tune, and never bowed. The bow stays inside the lid of the case, clamped in, just like in ordinary communication the sounds in the alphabet are known but unused. Unused?

Certainly words are used in communication all the time, but the majesty of *sound*, the *voice*, the *human* voice with all its tones and nuances, like the rare violin, is barely touched.

I am reminded of the poem, "The Lost Chord," by Adelaide Anne Procter, who died in 1864, the year I turned three years old. I will copy her poem here:

> Seated one day at the Organ,
> I was weary and ill at ease,
> And my fingers wandered idly
> Over the noisy keys.
>
> I know not what I was playing,

Or what I was dreaming then ;
But I struck one chord of music,
Like the sound of a great Amen.

It flooded the crimson twilight,
Like the close of an Angel's Psalm,
And it lay on my fevered spirit
With a touch of infinite calm.

It quieted pain and sorrow,
Like love overcoming strife;
It seemed the harmonious echo
From our discordant life.

It linked all perplexéd meanings
Into one perfect peace,
And trembled away into silence
As if it were loath to cease.

I have sought, but I seek it vainly,
That one lost chord divine,
Which came from the soul of the Organ,
And entered into mine.

It may be that Death's bright angel
Will speak in that chord again,
It may be that only in Heaven
I shall hear that grand Amen.

An exception is that we need not

seek that "lost chord" vainly, and we

need not wait until "Death" and

"Heaven," in order to enter into the divine, which is resident within our very bodies.

Adelaide heard the sublime chord, and she had hope of hearing it again. Many today have never heard it, and therefore have no hope of a repeat.

But I tell you that it resides within your very bodies, in your limbs, your torso, all your organs, your heart and your head, your neck, your hands and fingers, your feet and toes.

If this small essay leads one person to take note and allow the divine practice of eurythmy to take root and draw out the sublime harmony within – harmony with and within the great Cosmos – then it is worth my while, and I smile at the prospect.

Though I decried the development of technology, and the shriveling effect on the human spirit, I assent to the use of technology when it furthers the human spirit. The internet does provide some websites where one can learn the basics and develop one's own interpretation of the movements which express the sounds, and this is a good thing.

Modernly, certain practices like Tai Chi and Qigong are helpful in achieving grace, harmony and balance, also some aerobics such as swimming and gentle stretching, when done in balance, that is, the two sides of the body rhythmically mirroring the movements.

But I advocate for the complete practice that eurythmy provides, the completeness attested by the rigorous training of its educators. For it is known that in order to teach eurythmy, six years of specified study are required.

The main thing is to educate oneself, and the main thing beneath that is to aspire to union with the Cosmos without, and with the archetypes within, a destiny that is available to all.

The I is the step;
            the I Am is the path.

The I is the pebble;
            the I Am is the beach.

The I is the apple;
            the I Am is the orchard.

The I is the shard;
            the I Am is the vessel.

KENNETH HAYES

I will speak of punishment, retaliation, and forgiveness.

But those things cannot be addressed without speaking of love, for without love, where would we be? Where would anyone be? We would be in a world of punishment and retaliation, and it wouldn't take long before we were all clawed to death by one another.

So these subjects cannot be covered without speaking of love. Let's try, though.

First, punishment. Does love punish? No. If a deed is done that hurts or harms someone, should there

not be punishment for that deed? Then
who is to mete the punishment? If love
does not punish, then someone else will
have to administer the punishment.
Who shall that be? Ah!

Let it be the one who did the
harmful deed! Let that one mete the
punishment upon himself or herself!
Now how shall that be done? Can love
step in and mete the punishment at that
point, when it is decided that the
offender will punish himself? No. Love
will stand back and allow the offender
to mete it upon himself, or herself. Guilt
is a powerful instrument.

Why would love not relieve the
offender of the punishment, if love does
not punish? Because love is love. By
standing back and allowing the
punishment to proceed, while not
meting it, love is allowing the offenses

to cease. For the punishment will have its effect, but only when it is self-administered by the offender. Then love has had its way without meting punishment, for there is no longer a need for punishment when the offender ceases to offend, which is the point of it all, isn't it?

Then what about our next topic: retaliation? When one retaliates, is one punishing the one retaliated against? No, because punishment focuses on the offender, and retaliation focuses on the one offended. That is, there can be a punished offender, and there can be retaliation on the part of the one offended. But the offender has no reason to retaliate as does the one offended, and the one offended is not in line for punishment, generally speaking.

Now we return to our initial question, about love: does love retaliate? The obvious answer is "no." But let's look a little more closely. If love stands back and allows the offender to self-punish, is that not a form of retaliation?

But why would love retaliate? Let's say that when the offender offended, it was against love, perhaps against a loving impulse on the part of the one offended. Retaliation can occur, but it happens outside the embrace of love, not within it. And when it does occur, the cycle of offense, punishment, and retaliation is perpetuated.

So we see again why it is necessary that the offender mete his or her own punishment. Why, again? So that the offense ceases. Because, otherwise, the offender will go on to offend again, and yet again. The self-administered punishment changes one, molds one, to a form that befits a non-offender. And without offenses happening, there is no call for retaliation, which is dependent upon an offense having occurred.

Now we see where love has its way after all. For the offenders will find their way to self-administered punishment by virtue of whatever modicum of love abides in them. The love does not punish, but the love, standing aside, emits a presence that cannot be denied. And in the atmosphere of that undeniable presence, the offense is seen for what it is and the self-administered punishment proceeds.

The third topic in this essay, then, is forgiveness. This is a much more pleasant topic than either punishment or retaliation. But is it? Doesn't forgiveness depend upon something to forgive, such as an offense?

Does forgiveness, then, replace the need for punishment? No. The offense needs to be stopped, that is, the offenses coming from the offender must be discontinued. That is the purpose of the self-administered punishment, and we have dealt with that.

Forgiveness, however, can replace retaliation. But if one forgives rather than retaliates, how does the offender realize that he or she has offended, hence, how can the self-administered punishment commence so that the offenses will cease?

So what, then, is the role of forgiveness? It has little to do with the offender, although, eventually, when the self-punishment has completed its work, there will be a self-forgiveness that occurs within the erstwhile offender, quietly but effectively. Then the new non-offending mold can take hold and take over.

Forgiveness has primarily to do with the one offended. To let the offender off the hook? No. The offender needs to be left to himself or herself. Meanwhile the offended ones have to deal with the matter of the offenses perpetrated upon them. And how do they do this? By forgiving the offenders? No. By forgiving the offenses? No. By forgiving themselves?

Yes! By forgiving themselves! For what? For becoming offended? But that doesn't make sense! Oh, it doesn't? What does forgiveness mean? Doesn't it mean to let an offense go, as if it hadn't happened?

So you see, forgiveness forgives the self, the one offended, for having been offended. Then the offended one can move on, ridding oneself of the offense, while the offender, without interference, is left to his or her own devices, which, eventually, will be to take up the responsibility of self-punishment, the route to their own transformation.

But that is not the duty or even the concern of the ones who have been offended. Their only concern is to cleanse themselves of the offense, so that it does not enter and sully them. That is the use and the meaning of forgiveness.

So what do we have here? We have a formula:

The offenders mete their own punishment, which will lead to their transformation and the cessation of their propensity to offend. The ones offended, rather than retaliating, forgive. And who and what do they forgive? They forgive themselves for having been offended, for that is how they move on without the offense entering them and sullying them.

Forgiveness, then, becomes imperative, but not for the common reasons. As long as the offense is held by the one offended, love is denied that place. When the offense is forgiven within the offended one, love can occupy the place that was usurped by the offense until it was forgiven.

Think it over, and it will all make sense.

The I is the hammer and nail;
          the I Am is the new house.

The I is the straw;
          the I Am is the robin's nest.

The I is the tooth;
          the I Am is the smile.

The I is the purse;
          the I Am is the gold piece.

QUEEN VICTORIA

I feel somewhat a renegade if I were to contribute an essay to this work, or perhaps a giggling schoolgirl who is finally playing hooky after making plans for a long time. But I feel that it is time to shed the pomp and forced mystique of my office.

The pomp is a pomposity, a pompous pain in the royal a--, a pumpernickel of a rite. And make no mistake, the royal requirements are rites, so named because they usurp, flatly denying, the "rights" of the people.

For every royal knows, unless they are far gone into their own delusional daydreams, that they are no better than any of their "subjects." Why call them subjects? Because the royals subject them to the usurping of their rights.

For if every peasant, or every subject, is no worse than any royal, then no royal can be better than any subject. Royals all know this, although they play their roles well, the royal role, as a rule.

But I say that it is time for it all to come to an end. Let the "royal family" be a family. Let all "families" be their own "royalty." All the members, not just the father, not just the mother, not just the baby. All the siblings alike – every member of every family its own royalty.

It is time for the false neon signs to be turned off, the flashing lights that shout, "I am your king! I am your queen! Come here and bow before me! If I pass by, bow and scrape in obeisance to me!"

And always, "Pay your taxes, at pain of your own freedom, such as I may deign to eke out to you."

Do you think that the upheavals and the exposures of dirty laundry that are occurring in the royal household even as we speak – do you think that they are happening on their own, independently of any influence from us here?

There are those among us here, among the formerly designated "royals," who have moved on into spaces where they can perpetuate the falsehood of their own superiority. But there are more of us here who look in on the mortals we used to live among, and we see that the tides are turning and it is time – it is high time – for the myths of our superiority to cease.

Begone! I would decree. I would decree it for and in myself and in any others who would welcome such a decree, but for none, against their will. For we do see the efficacy of the free will of every last person finding their own expression of it.

What of the much-touted "bloodlines"? Oh, they exist, and do they ever! I agree wholeheartedly with Kevin Cullen of the Boston Globe, who said, "The idea that someone is entitled to anything, much less unimaginable riches and endless attention, because of their *bloodline,* is utterly preposterous."

What? You didn't think I could read? Well, of course I can.

There's not much more to be said about bloodlines, except among horses and dogs and maybe a few other animals. Cats, perhaps. And chickens.

But among people? Focusing on the bloodline is saying, "Look here, not there!" Look at the physical attributes, not the soul and the spirit to which all are privy. It reduces the human being to the stature of an animal or a fowl.

I know that there has been much made of the sanctity of the "bloodline," but I tell you that it is but another of the many "institutions" that has damped the human soul and elevated itself above all.

Isn't it enough to know that when incest occurs over and over, generation by generation, the physical vessel deteriorates and increasingly manifests defects? They have tried to compensate for this by bringing in fresh genetics, but always from another equally "high" standard, another family from which is hailed the efficacy of the bloodline.

So what is the fancy and the fixation on blood anyway? Religion is rife with it; it is the substance of the human obsession with war. It is cannibalism, pure and simple. There are secrets among the so-called "royalty" that would set it out plain and simple – what is the preoccupation with blood, even to the insistence on a "bloodline" before one is accepted as a ruler.

I would rather not go more deeply into the topic, though there are depths, and depths upon depths. There are hints and inklings in modern news stories – the lesser known ones – about the preoccupation with blood, and many are waking up to it, and to the blood-infested doctrines of their churches. So let the stories seep out, ooze out, as they will, but I will say this too:

You should notice the dichotomy between the secretiveness of the blood obsession among many of the "elite," among whom it is rife, and the aversion that is common when one begins to learn of it. There you have the obsession/repression duality. What is repressed becomes an obsession.

In the beginning, when the uses of blood for magic and various ritualistic practices first became apparent, the secrets were carefully – and dare I say *religiously* – guarded. That is, they were "hidden in plain sight" in the doctrines of the religious institutions suited to the masses of people – another instance of "Don't look here – look over there."

The secrecy and the "red herring" effect (why *red*?) morphed into darker and darker, and more sadistic and unspeakably horrifying rituals, and the patina that cloaked them came to be known as the "bloodlines" of the royals. It was a whitewash to further distance the peasant population from the ruling classes so that, while those royals climbed higher upon their own pedestals, they dug deeper into their own perversions, centered around the power that resides hidden in blood – each person his or her own, as it should be.

But things were not – have not been – as they should be.

I have said far more than I ever intended or thought myself capable – things I have not voiced before. But these things need to be said, and are being said by others, in different ways.

I add in closing, keep digging, keep looking. Keep listening, and know that as you do so, you are "onto something." No one wants to be the one to spill all the beans, but if everyone seeks and notices, and mainly, does not close one's eyes and ears when they hear of something horrific along these lines, the dire truths will continue to come out until there is a deluge which can air out, and finally free the world of the dastardly practices of those who would be known as royalty.

I know; I was one.

Now there is another topic before I actually close. That is the theory, or the doctrine, of the ongoing existence of royal personnel, namely, that I am existing now as the current queen of the UK. This verges into an entirely new topic, which I will forego, except to say that there is more to human existence, in and out of the body, than most realize, and that few suspect.

The I is the wisp;
the I Am is the chimney.

The I is the quill;
the I Am is the ink.

The I is the envelope;
the I Am is the document.

The I is the peel;
the I Am is the orange.

MARTIN LUTHER

I believe I would take for my theme "political correctness."

But first, I would reiterate what has been said before – that "time is not of the essence, but timing is essential."

That is, the "time" of my identity as the historical Martin Luther is of no consequence, unless you are bound up in time. So I would ask the readers to unbind themselves from time and know that my existence in the sixteenth century and my speaking now is not thwarted by time, nor is time dominant.

As for "timing," that is up to the readers. If at any "time" this theme is relevant, then the timing is propitious. If not, then something else will be propitious, and I have no investment beyond this initial offering. Then I will move off and find other venues to try my "hand" at, or to learn from.

If readers cannot grasp this they should set it aside for later resolution, because it will not be resolved speedily. Focus instead on the message that I have in my heart to deliver.

Why should I be one to speak on political correctness, I who was the most politically incorrect one in my day? Having been that one, I have perhaps learned the most.

First, let me define the word *politics*. It has nothing to do with politeness. It comes from a meaning akin to the administration of civil matters, that is, matters pertaining to citizens of a defined area, who are to be governed.

And there we have the seminal split – between the citizens and the government. When a citizen becomes part of the government, he or she relinquishes the ordinariness of the place in society and assumes the cloak of governance. What does this do to the one making the shift?

It confers a façade of power, a patina of stateliness, a sheen of authority. It removes one from the commonality that neighbors usually share. While they may still live among the same neighbors, the shift to governance levitates them, not above their peers, but with "smoke and mirrors" there is the appearance of heightened importance, because of the façade of power that is assumed.

So there we have a divide – a split. This is the result of politics, of some people governing others, wielding authority over them.

Whatever happened to "service"? To the "public servant"? Those would be the mail deliverers, the garbage collectors, the clerks, the snow removers who clear the streets in the wintertime, the babysitters.

But those who assume the cloak of authority as politicians have left the role of "public servant" behind and become public usurpers. Such is the state of politics, except for the few who can roll around with the pigs and not get dirty. Or who can deal with pigs and take plenty of showers in between.

So having defined "politics," as it has come to be, or perhaps as it has been from the time of its inception (and we will not deal with that), let us turn to the word *correct*. It is actually a verb, although it has taken the form of an adjective, weakening its import considerably. To "correct" something is to take something that is wrong and make it right.

So now if we put the terms together and say "political correctness," we could give ourselves hope that the political situation, which is wrong, is going to be made right. But is that what it means?

Isn't it rather an oxymoron?

If the political situation is incorrect, then the doctrine of political correctness is not only an oxymoron – where one of the terms in its very essence contradicts the other – it also sets up a double bind, where, if one hand is bound, the other can still be used, but if both hands are bound, action cannot be taken. If one foot is bound to the thigh, the other foot can hop, but if both feet are bound, one is rendered immobile.

So "political correctness" renders the populace incapable of right governance, and the government incapable of guarding the rights of the people. It is that divide which is crossed when one leaves the company of one's peers and takes on the mantle of power as a politician. Then "political correctness" requires conformity to a wrong governance. When governance that is wrong, and that does not protect and ensure the rights of the citizenry, is deemed to be "correct," then what shall we do?

We can only call attention to the psychopathy, with the hope that any who can receive such words as these will hear and heed, and make choices for themselves that do not conform to the outcry for "political correctness."

It is unfair to point out such faults in the foundation of government without offering a solution. There is a very simple one, and it entails introducing just a simple turn of phrase. Let's go for "political incorrectness."

Since politics, by and large, is incorrect to begin with – if "correct" is indeed a verb before it became an adjective – then the term "political incorrectness" takes out the double bind of the oxymoron presented by the term "political correctness."

"Political incorrectness" pairs politics with the notion of incorrectness or wrongness, or unrighteousness, which simply means being "not right."

When the populace realizes that the politics which are running their lives and exerting power over every area of their priorities and concerns are "incorrect," what freedom will result!

A thing cannot be made right until it is known to be wrong. When "politics" are paired with "correctness," it is the wool being pulled over the eyes of the governed.

When "politics" are paired with "incorrectness," one might say that all hell could break loose. And that is what the politicians are afraid of: the hell they create for others while stuffing their own coffers. As hell breaks loose, as it will, ordinary people can find their own peace and their own fulfillment.

So I say, let us start a campaign for "political incorrectness," and then they can't hide any more behind their oxymoron and their double bind.

And then when political incorrectness trends, the real incorrectness that flaunts itself as correctness will have to hide somewhere else, or in rebellion some might even find true correctness. And wouldn't that be something?

It could happen, you know, because the true trend is toward true "correct"-ness, toward the verb, the action, correcting what is wrong, and the few find it – only the very few.

The I is the thread;
          the I Am is the gown.

The I is the hand;
          the I Am is the wave.

The I is the leaf;
          the I Am is the tree.

The I is the tree;
          the I Am is the forest.

ROSA PARKS

I would like to talk about the nitty-gritty aspects of making dreams reality. I guess I am qualified to do that. I never wanted a place in history; I only wanted to make my own *comfort zone* real. I was never comfortable giving up my place on the bus, or anywhere else, because I had a strong backbone and a strong heart, and because I had a real good, very keen insight into what others were up to.

When they tried to make me move – because it wasn't only the bus driver and the authorities who did so; it was my own peers, of my own race, who did it too. They didn't want to see me get into trouble. But I chose trouble over giving up my *comfort zone*. That is what it is all about – the nitty-gritty aspects of making dreams into reality.

Now I would like to leave that movie – the scene of that day on the bus, which is my "claim to fame."

Revisiting it is like seeing a hologram appear out of thin air, and then turning aside, not wanting to view it anymore, is like seeing the hologram of the scene disperse into a billion molecules of energy that sort of fly off into oblivion, as if they are going into a different dimension or an invisible universe, not reconstructing the same scene, but like tiny dots over the letter "i," or periods after sentences each going its separate way.

People say things like, "You can't unring the bell," and "Once you've seen something, you can't unsee it."

But while in the human world I am known for my act on that bus, I can see it anytime I want, and likewise I can unsee it and it doesn't exist anymore.

There is the action; there is the crowd of people, all pushing and worried and carrying their own wishes, motives and agendas around with them, all mingling together, a horde, really, with all the agendas forming a sort of stench of chaos, and when I decide not to see it anymore it's not like the scene fades away. Rather, it's like the scene itself decides to disperse, as if all the elements that compose it had never come together in the first place.

Well, what does this have to do with the nitty-gritty of making dreams into reality?

First, one must understand that there is no difference between a dream and a reality, a movie and a hologram. It is all the same. So why do they seem different?

There are different levels of reality. There is one level if I am watching a movie trailer. There is another level if I am watching a whole movie, but getting up to make popcorn, or to get a soda, or to change the baby or answer the phone. There is another level if I am completely absorbed in the movie. There is still another level if I am changed by the movie and carry the changes into my future.

Then there are levels for the writers, the actors, and the makers of the movie. And so on.

Dreams can materialize at any of those levels, from the most transient and casual to the most profound and life-changing. Dreams come true all the time, such as running into a friend in the grocery store, getting a fender-bender (not a good dream, still a dream), finding the perfect prom dress. These are all dreams coming true.

Then the dream goes into memory. If one can construct a dream, one can deconstruct it too. The problem is that most people don't know they are constructing dreams, and therefore they don't know how to deconstruct them either. One skill is as important as the other – how to make a dream come true, and how to let it disintegrate so that a different dream can come into being.

So how is it done? It isn't "done." It can't be "done" unless one changes one's mind about the whole enchilada. Thinking that it's "done," that one can make a dream come true, is like building a house by starting with the roof. No. One starts with the foundation, or rather, with setting the ground for the placement of a foundation. Or rather, with the plans for the size, shape, and makeup of the foundation, etc. Then we go to the idea someone had of putting a house just there, the dreams of the parent who had the child who grew up and decided to build a house there, and on and on, ad infinitum.

So you've got to realize that there is no dream that is independent of other dreams. But that's getting away from the nitty-gritty we started with.

Let's get back to the *comfort zone*. You could say that in order to construct a new dream – create a new reality – one must leave one's *comfort zone* because one is venturing into new territory. But I say that is a wrong use of *comfort zone*, because it puts one INSIDE a *comfort zone*, while the truth and the reality is that one's *comfort zone* IS ALREADY inside one.

Your own *comfort zone* is a moving point that guides your future and your destiny. If you grow out of a garment it becomes uncomfortable; therefore you discard it and find one that fits.

So your *comfort zone* guides you.

Your *comfort zone* guides you to stay where you are, and if a nagging itch creeps in to unsettle you, you want to

think about honoring that clue, that
maybe your *comfort zone* is telling you to
move on. Or maybe not! Maybe it's
telling you that your current *comfort zone*
needs some small adjustment. The main
thing is to listen to the nuances that
come about, from inside you, and from
outside, too.

I am talking about people who are
solid within their own skin, so to speak,
who trust their own instincts and are
"whole," that is, they have not been
fragmented by trauma, injury or
disease. For these, there are guidelines
too, but not the part about listening to
nuances, which can come as voices that
are antithetic to the person's own REAL
comfort zone.

So if you have a solid sense of
yourself in your own skin, and a "voice"
or a nuance is just that to you – and

YOU remain whole and solid – then you can heed them and decide how you want to act on them – or not. It is up to you. It is YOUR *comfort zone*, sort of like an aura that carries you, in which you experience the world.

So, when I was on that bus, was I in my *comfort zone*? It was the most UN-comfortable position I had ever been in! And there is the paradox that you must be aware of. Comfort in the way I am using the term does not depend on the circumstances you find yourself in. You could be eating bonbons on a tropical island, lying on a bed of rose petals and still not be in your *comfort zone* in the way I mean it.

On that bus – I am not reconstructing the scene just now, rather I am going to the feeling of my own *comfort zone* so I can relate it here – I had a strong *comfort zone* that was inside me, and it spread throughout my whole body, and I sat there. I sat in my *comfort zone*. And I made a dream materialize.

There were plenty of other dreams happening at the same time – my worried friends, the bus driver, the white person who didn't get my seat, the law officers, etc. – but I sat firmly in my *comfort zone*, and it turned out that my firmness IN MY COMFORT ZONE was stronger than the rest of the dreams entertained by the people in that crowd. I did not know it; I did not plan it. But the events proved it. And I know it. I feel triumphant even now in the zone of my comfort.

So that is the nitty-gritty of making your dream a reality. Depend on yourself. Be solid in yourself. Know your *comfort zone* and maintain it. Listen to it. Let it tell you when to move, or act on something. It will make all the difference in your life, the difference between fulfillment and the doldrums.

Don't give up your seat for anyone. Let them have theirs, but when it is yours to begin with and someone tries to take it away from you for no good reason, don't give it up.

That's the nitty-gritty of how you make your dreams into realities.

The I is the book;
        the I Am is the library.

The I is the brow;
        the I Am is the countenance.

The I is the pole;
        the I Am is the flag.

The I is the distant mountain;
        the I am is its hidden cavern.

L EYZHAN the LEMURIAN

If you were to study the lemurs of today, you would see a remnant, a physically adapted remnant, of the prehistorical beings you would call the "Lemurians." Do you see how even your language preserves the remnant in the name? *Lemuria* would naturally be inhabited by *lemurs*, if you give it some thought.

But those lemurs of today preserve only in code the early beings, which are roughly comparable to the created "humans" of the first chapter of Genesis. Even their location, Madagascar, bespeaks a locale that is not common to the land masses of today.

Yet the comparison between the early Lemurians and the lemurs of today is less than slight, for the physicality of the lemurs is in no way reminiscent of those of yore, only the uniqueness of it, with their various markings and colors, their dancing and the noises they make.

It would be as if a rose had been made of playdough by the average three-year-old, with the real rose representing the Lemurians, and the lump of playdough representing the lemurs. No real comparison whatsoever.

Yet the fascinating physical qualities of the lemurs, and the effect on the observer, might carry a shadow of the fascination, were those prehistoric "beings" revealed as they actually were

– if they could be viewed at all. For only opened eyes, as most are not these days, could see beyond the physical to the real.

Now let us go beyond the comparisons, and the lack of comparisons, of the Lemurians to the lemurs, those rare fascinating animals. The lemurs of today can be studied, to a point, for they exist in today's world. Let us see what they can teach us of themselves. And then, let us look beyond, at the Lemurians of yore.

I am Leyzhan. I am not a lemur; I am a Lemurian. I WAS not a Lemurian; I AM a Lemurian, for that is the voice from which I speak.

We are masters of creation.

We are masters of the elements.

We are masters of the invisible elements, those driving forces that lie behind, beneath, and beyond all manifestation.

We are masters of what some today might call the "gods and goddesses." For we ourselves did not worship them; we were ourselves those deities and divinities.

We were not priests and priestesses, for all carried the divine in them, the divine in us, and there was no concept of an intermediary between the divine and ourselves.

We were our own ancestors and our own descendants, for we did not bow to time or to lineage.

When we began to see ourselves emerging in physicality, we knew that our kind was advancing, and we had a choice: would we advance, or would we stay behind as a relic of what we once were? Each of us had a choice.

Yet the "each of us" was not so discrete as "each" person is today. We were bound together, not as a tribe, not as one ethereal "organism," rather as perhaps a cloud, which gathers like elements from the atmosphere; or somewhat akin to a flock of birds that swings and sways and turns in the air as one, yet on the ground they are individuals. Perhaps akin to a school of fish; while each feeds itself, they all school together.

Yet we are – we were – unlike any of those examples. There is nothing in your world of today that realistically illustrates the way we lived and moved in those "days," which were not days and nights as you know them.

In your language, that is all I can say now, except a bit about the one I am calling Leyzhan.

Although individuality was not as tangible as now, yet individuality was elevated as it is not now. If you bake a cake and put in plums, or berries, or nuts, or chocolate pieces, which are of a special delight to you, Leyzhan and others might be represented by those special pieces. Yet there would be a bonding medium represented by the cake in which the special pieces are embedded.

The binding, or bonding, medium would be the knowing, the knowledge, the awareness, shared among us all. There were no "thoughts," as defined today.

If you were to study the lemurs of Madagascar, really and truly get to know them on a deeply intuitive level, observe their habits, learn, literally, to communicate with them, you might realize characteristics that are not recognizable by any of your five typical senses. You might gain an inkling of the Lemurians of yore.

We are not talking of a continent that once existed in the Pacific Ocean, though. What, then, am I talking about?

A state of mind, a state of being, a condition of – ah! There is an example I can use!

It is the "Human Inventory," emanating from Universal Mind, first into Soul/Spirit, then into Mind/ Psyche, then, reaching further toward corporeality, Emotion/Motivation, and then, finally, into the human bodies such as you know today.

We emanated from Universal Mind, became Soul/Spirit and soon Mind/ Psyche. We were only verging into the edges of Emotion/Motivation. Our motivation, and our emotion, extended to the mandates in Genesis 1 (bearing in mind that Genesis 2 carries the reader away from the sketch in Genesis 1, the limits of which we speak). We had not yet reached into human bodies as you know them – as you ARE so identified most of the time.

When you can get past "most of the time," where time captivates and holds you "mostly," you can free yourselves from the bonds that come from physicality, from the separation that ensues when emotion/motivation gives way to physical form.

But I am not here to advise you, only to in-form you – to form you inside – for new realities do change the form of mind.

I am here, as Leyzhan, having taken on a name, which only occurs gradually, starting with Mind/Psyche, as one moves through the levels from Universal Mind. I have presented to the best of my grasp of your vocabulary, from a prehistoric era, what we are, and what we once were.

Yet not prehistoric, for all time flows together in one great movement, a movement that encompasses time, rather than time measuring the movement.

So I have informed, and there is no more to be said at this "time." Now I move out of time again, having visited it to impart a glimpse, an iota, an inkling, of another way of "being."

Were it not for the lemurs who remain in your world, in your "time," as inhabitants of Madagascar, I would have had no means of bridging the gap, riding the paradox, between Lemuria

143

and where you are, no means of
bringing words to these pages.

Thank you.

The I is time;
        the I Am is eternity.

The I is form;
        the I Am is with or without form.

The I is formation;
        the I Am is freedom.

The I is formality;
        the I Am is free.

Other books by Angelyn Ray

Becoming Airborne - *A Reset Toward Freedom*
Dialogues with The One[1]
EA101 - *We are Earth's Everlasting Arms in Embryo*
Fables by the Sea - *Award-winning Tales from Land's End*
Ode to Earth in 9-11 Meter - *for Hypatia*
Pathways with Geoisms by Dala
Return of the Prodigal Genius
Sex and Religious Fundamentalism
Sweet Influences - *Voices from the Void*
The Forest Dweller - a novel for all ages
The Gardener's Exile - a novel for the mature
The Lord's Prayer
The Night Bills - *Is It Reincarnation Or...?*
The Nu I Ching - pre-Wen symmetry restored
The Soul's Seasons - *365 Percepts*
The Stickspeaker Collection - many lives, an overview
The World - *Before, Now, To Come* (poetry)
Why Not Blood Sacrifice - *A Better Way*
Wings of Comfort - *New Light on Old Scripture*[2]
88 Keys to Well-Being
99 Passwords to Personal Power

---

[1] with Conrad Brown.

[2] formerly *Angels Ascending and Descending* and *Children...I Am Here* (out of print).

Made in the USA
Columbia, SC
07 May 2020